FOR INFORMATION:
Impact Publishing, LLC
PO Box 74610
Baton Rouge, LA 70874

SPEAK to it!

Changing Your Life with the POWER of Your Words

RODNEY D. ROBERTSON
LESTER E. DALE JR.

Impact|Publishing
Impacting your world with inspiration™
BATON ROUGE, LA

SPEAK to it!

contents

Contents

introduction

YOUR WORDS HAVE POWER! IT took me a long time to figure out that my words have power and that I was experiencing the fruit of my own spoken words. For years, I experienced defeat and failure because of my wrong confession. However, one day I had an "aha moment" and I realized that I possessed in my life what I had been confessing. **In my mouth and in your mouth, lies the power to change our lives and achieve victory over our circumstances through the power of spoken words.** Death and life lies in the power of our tongues. We have the creative ability to change our world and paint the canvas of our lives with spoken faith-filled words. *Our lives can become better by changing how we think and what we say about ourselves and our circumstances.*

It has been told that "you are what you eat" and this is very true as it relates to our health and knowing our bodies. In addition, I believe in a spiritual principle that says "you are what you speak" or "you have whatever you say" (Mark 11:23). **Words are containers of power that have the creative ability to take on the form of what you say whether it is negative or positive.** Right now, your life is filled with the things that you have spoken. For example, if you've been confessing (speaking) that every time I get money in my hands, something comes up to take it. Guess what? You are right and you have what you say. Every time you get money something will come up to devour your money. Why, because you have what you say.

In this book, we want to help you get positive results for your life, family, ministry, and business by speaking the RIGHT words. You can change your life by taking control of what you think (your mind) and what you say (your mouth). **What you say about yourself and circumstances do matter.** You and I have the power to either bless our futures or curse our futures. It is up to us. We must make sure the words we speak or send out into the atmosphere are in the direction we want our lives, ministry, or business to go in. It is time to speak FAITH-FILLED words that can change your life and circumstances. We are not victims. We are victors and have the power to frame our world with the power of our words.

Get ready to be empowered to take charge of your life and circumstances through the power of faith confessions. You no longer have to allow your circumstances to dictate your lifestyle and hold you bondage. It is your time to conquer your world through faith and live the abundant life that God has promised you.

PART I

The Heart of the Matter

Faith in the Heart

Above all else, guard your heart,
for it affects everything you do.

Proverbs 4:23 NLT

Believe with the Heart...

The heart of man is the spirit of man. The human spirit is God's contact point in which He illuminates and reveals (Prov. 20:27). Man (human race) is made up of three parts i.e., spirit, soul, and body. Man is a (speaking) spirit; he possesses a soul (mind, will, and emotions), and lives in a body. The Bible says that with the HEART one believes unto righteousness, and with the mouth confession is made unto salvation (Rom.10:10). It is with the heart that one believes and it is with the mouth that one confesses (says the same thing God says). **Faith must begin first in your heart.** Let's look at Mark 11:23. It says, "For assuredly, I say to you, whoever, says to this mountain, 'Be removed and be cast into the sea,' and does not doubt in his HEART, but believes that those things he says will be done, he will have whatever he says." It is with the HEART that one believes.

When the Bible speaks of believing with your "heart," it isn't referring to the human organ in your chest cavity or that which pumps blood throughout your body. If that was the case, then we would believe God with our bodies. The word "heart" in the above Scripture doesn't refer to the human heart. It refers to the core, center of man and that is his spirit. When one believes with his heart, he is believing with his spirit. Again, man is a (speaking) spirit; he possesses a soul (mind, will, and emotions), and lives in a body.

Before You Start Confessing...

Before we can get to a positive faith confession, we must understand that faith begins in the heart. Why, because the heart affects everything we do. In fact, the book of Proverbs admonishes us to guard our hearts because it affects everything we do (Prov.4:23 NLT). We must guard our hearts against doubt, fear, strife, unforgiveness, bitterness, etc. because those things will hinder the manifestation of what we are believing God for in our lives.

You can only produce what you have deposited in your heart.

A good man out of the good treasure of the heart brings forth good things and an evil man out of the evil treasure brings forth evil things (Matt.12:35). In the Greek, another word for treasure in this verse is "deposit." It could read like this, "A good man out of the good DEPOSIT of the heart brings forth good things and an evil man out of the evil DEPOSIT brings forth evil things." **You can only produce what you have deposited in your heart.** Your heart is the manufacturer for your words, fears, faith, miracles, madness, breakthrough, break-down, peace, or blessings. Whether it is positive or negative it begins in your heart. **You can only produce what's in your heart.** What's in your heart? What are you feeding on? Your spiritual diet will affect the condition of your heart. *Whatever is in your heart in excess will show up in your life.*

Before you can speak faith-filled words or have a positive faith confession, your heart (spirit) must first be filled with faith-filled words. Why, because the mouth can only speak what the heart has received. In fact, the Scripture says that out of the abundance (surplus or superabundance) of the heart the mouth speaks (Matt.12:34). **Whatever is in our hearts in surplus is what is going to come out of our mouths.** Whether it is worry, doubt, fear, or faith; whatever is overflowing in your heart will flow out of your mouth. Therefore, your heart determines what your mouth will say.

*Whatever is in our hearts in surplus
is what is going to come out
of our mouths.*

Faith Food for the Heart...

If you and I are going to have a believing heart that is filled with faith, we must tap into the source of faith. Jesus said that man shall not live by bread (that which is temporal) alone, but by EVERY WORD that proceeds out of the mouth of God (Matt.4:4). **The Word of God is the faith food for a believing heart.** The Word of God is the source for your faith to increase. It is spiritual food to your spirit as natural food is to your body. The Word is the sustenance of your faith.

A few years ago, I hired a personal trainer because I wanted to get fit and increase my muscle mass. One of the things my trainer told me was to increase my protein intake. If I was going to "bulk up" or increase my muscle mass, I had to increase my protein intake. Likewise, if we are going to increase our faith (muscle), we must increase our intake of the Word of God (protein). The more Word you hear and put in your heart; the more your faith will increase and develop.

So then faith comes by hearing and hearing by the Word of God (Rom.10:17). Faith comes by hearing and hearing and hearing again. When you and I give a listening ear to the Word of God, faith comes. What we repeatedly hear affects what we believe. **Faith responds to the WORD and God responds to faith.** Without faith, it is impossible to please God (Heb.11:6). Our God is a faith God. What brings him pleasure is when we have faith (trust and rely solely) on him.

Therefore, if you and I want to please God or make him happy, we must have faith in him. We must believe that he is able to do exceedingly, abundantly and above what we can ask or think. Have faith in God. It's not faith in faith, but FAITH IN GOD that moves mountains and empowers us to live the overcoming life.

Faith responds to the Word and God responds to faith.

Faith is a by-product of the Word. It comes by hearing and hearing the Word over and over again. "My child, pay attention to what I say. Listen carefully to my words. Don't lose sight of them. Let them penetrate deep into your heart, for they bring life to those who find them, and healing to their whole body. Guard your heart above all else, for it determines the course of your life" (Proverbs 4:20-23 NLT).

Give attention to what God says. His words are spirit and they are life. The Word has the ability to bring healing to your body. The Word is the source from which your faith grows. The Word is the fertilizer for the ground of your heart. Guard your heart and fill it with the Word because it determines the course of your life.

FAITH REMINDERS...

- ◀ In my mouth and in your mouth, lies the power to change our lives and achieve victory over our circumstances through the power of spoken words.
- ◀ Words are containers of power that have the creative ability to take on the form of what you say whether it is negative or positive.
- ◀ What you say about yourself and circumstances do matter.
- ◀ Faith must begin first in your heart.
- ◀ You can only produce what you have deposited in your heart.
- ◀ Whatever is in our hearts in surplus is what is going to come out of our mouths.
- ◀ Faith responds to the WORD and God responds to faith.
- ◀ Faith is a by-product of the Word.

Make it Personal:
What I learned about faith is...

____

____

____

____

____

____

____

____

____

____

____

____

____

____

____

____

PART II

The Power of Spoken Faith

EFFECTIVE FAITH

*That the sharing of your faith
may become effective by the
acknowledgment of every good thing
which is in you in Christ Jesus.*

PHILEMON 1:6 NKJV

Effective Faith...

Death and life lies in the power of our tongues (Pvb.18:21). Our words are either poison or healthy fruit. We must learn to say what God has said and live the victorious life that has been provided to us by Jesus Christ. We aren't believers trying to get the victory. We have the victory now in Christ and that victory must be reinforced through effective faith.

I like what Philemon 1:6 NKJV says, "*That the sharing of your faith may become effective by the acknowledgment of every good thing which is in you in Christ.*" My faith and your faith will become effective when we acknowledge the good things we have ALREADY in Christ. When we gave our lives to Christ, we inherited blessings and good things because of our identification with Christ.

*Your faith will never grow
beyond your confession.*

The tragedy for some believers is that they are more apt to acknowledge what's going wrong or what they lack instead of acknowledging what's theirs in Christ. Our salvation, peace, healing, deliverance, freedom, wholeness, breakthrough, wisdom, prosperity, victory, etc., is IN CHRIST. When you and I begin to acknowledge and talk about what we ALREADY have in Christ, our faith will become effective. This act of faith is very significant because your faith will never grow beyond your confession.

In Christ...

In Christ, you are ALL That! In fact, you look a lot better IN CHRIST than you do outside of Him. In Christ, you have been made the righteousness of God (2 Cor. 5:21). What does that mean you ask? It means you have been accepted and approved of by the Father. It means you have right standing with God. It means you have been made fit to enter into his presence. You are the righteousness of God in Christ!

If your faith is going to be effective, you must begin to acknowledge every good thing that is yours in Christ. The

Scripture didn't say "acknowledge what's going to be yours one day in Christ." It said that you should acknowledge the good things that are yours in Christ NOW.

The Amplified Bible says, "[And I pray] that the participation in and sharing of your faith may produce and promote full recognition and appreciation and understanding and precise knowledge of every good [thing] that is ours in [*our identification with*] Christ Jesus [and unto His glory]." Wow, every good thing that is ours is in our IDENTIFICATION with Christ Jesus.

You aren't waiting on victory. Victory is yours now in Christ (1 Cor.15:57)! You aren't waiting on wisdom. Wisdom is yours NOW (1 Cor. 1:30)! You must acknowledge and talk about what's yours in Christ. You aren't trying to get it. It is yours NOW!!

You have so much MORE working for you in Christ than you have working against you.

Your identity and inheritance is IN CHRIST! Before you acknowledge what you don't have, acknowledge what you do have in Christ. Before you acknowledge who you are not, acknowledge who you are in Christ. You have so much MORE working for you in Christ than you have working against you.

Another word for effective or effectual in the Greek is ACTIVE. So if we would use the word "active," it would read "That the sharing of your faith may become ACTIVE by the acknowledgment of every good thing which is in you in Christ." Wow, our faith becomes ACTIVE when we acknowledge every good thing that is ours in Christ.

Acknowledge every good thing that is yours in CHRIST and your faith will become active. Become more promise minded instead of problem minded. Live by the covenant you have with God and not your circumstances. The promises of God in Christ are yes and amen (2 Cor. 1:20). They are sure…GUARANTEED!

FAITH REMINDERS...

◀ Death and life lies in the power of the tongue (Proverbs 18:21).

◀ Your faith will become effective when you acknowledge the good things you have ALREADY in Christ.

◀ Your faith will never grow beyond your confession.

◀ Every good thing that is ours is in our IDENTIFICATION with Christ Jesus.

◀ You have so much MORE working for you in Christ than you have working against you.

Make it Personal:
What I learned about faith is...

3

Speak to IT

If you are not happy with what you have in life, you should check out what you have been saying.

[RDR]

Faith In Your Mouth...

Believers have mastered the believing part of faith; however, they are falling short in the speaking part of faith. Faith is voice activated. Faith must be in two places—in your heart and in your mouth. In 1973,

Charles Capps released a word of prophecy, *"If men would believe Me, long prayers are not necessary. Just speaking the Word will bring what you desire. My Word is not void of power. My people* are *void of speech."*

Faith must be in two places—
in your heart and in your mouth.

Faith must be in the heart (the Word believed) and in the mouth (the Word spoken). It's out of the abundance or surplus of the heart that the mouth will speak. Whatever (negative or positive) is placed in your heart will come up and out of your mouth. Your words are framing your world. In fact, you have in your life what you've been speaking into your life.

Mark 11:23 says, "For assuredly, I say to you, whoever SAYS to this mountain, 'Be removed and be cast into the sea,' and does not doubt in his heart, but believes that those things he SAYS will be done, he will have whatever he SAYS." In this verse, Jesus is speaking. He emphasizes speaking or 'says' three times more than 'believes.' By revelation of the Spirit, this lets us know that our speaking is very important. If you and I are going to be effective overcomers, we must say what God has said. We must speak to our mountain. Notice, Jesus didn't say climb it and it will move. He didn't say believe it and it will move. He didn't say think it and it will move. Why, because positive thinking only changes you and a faith confession changes your circumstances. Jesus told us to speak to the mountain. Open your mouth and say something. Tell the mountain (obstacle) where to go and it will obey you. You and I have been given power over our circumstances through the power of our words. You (whoever) will have whatever you say.

Believe and Speak...

Faith requires action and believing requires a confession. Your faith has to move your mouth. If your faith hasn't moved your mouth, then you have only mentally assented. The Scripture says, "We having the same spirit of faith, according as it is written, I BELIEVED, AND THEREFORE HAVE I SPOKEN; we also BELIEVE, and therefore SPEAK." (2 Cor.4:13)

Believing is only one part of faith. Jesus never said you will have what you believe; he said you will have whatever you say (Mark 11:23). Your life will be filled with the fruit of the words you've spoken. What are you speaking? What words are you reaping the results of? You may be one who has stopped saying negative words; however you haven't started speaking faith-filled words. If you aren't saying anything, you will lose by default. Rise up and speak what God has said about you, your life, and circumstances.

Positive thinking changes you. A faith confession changes your circumstances.

Positive thinking is good. You should work on your mind and develop right thinking. In fact, the Bible admonishes us to renew our minds and set our minds on those things that are true, noble, just, pure, lovely, and of a good report (Rom. 12:2; Phil. 4:8). However, as great as positive thinking is, it only changes you. A faith confession changes your circumstances. Within you and I, lies the creative power to change our circumstances and our lives. God is waiting on you to say something. He's waiting on you to speak his Word. We should say or decree and declare what God has already said. In fact, He said, "Just as you have spoken in My hearing, so I will do to you" (Numbers 14:28).

THE FIRST USE OF LANGUAGE...

The initial use of language was not communication but creativity. "Then God said, "Let there be light;" and there was light" (Gen. 1:3). Chaos was brought into life and order by the spoken words of God. All throughout this chapter, we see the creative power of God at work through the power of his words. God SAID and then he SAW. Sound preceded sight.

The worlds were framed by the Word of God and those things that we now see didn't come from anything that is visible (Heb. 11:3). The things we see now came from that which we can't see (WORDS). Likewise, we have the ability to frame and put in order our lives with the spoken Word of God. We can decree and declare a thing and it shall be established for us (Job 22:28). Even more, Isaiah reminds us that God will show us new things, hidden things [kept in reserve] that are called into being by the prophetic word (Isaiah 48:6-7 AMP).

God is waiting on us to call into being those things that are hidden to our natural sight into the earth realm. God has already spoken. Now, we must speak. We must decree a thing and it shall be established. We must say what God has said. Your victory is in your mouth. Your healing is in your mouth. Your breakthrough is in your mouth. Your success is in your mouth. Our words have the power to repel or attract what God has promised for our lives. Our faith confession has the power to bring us into possession. We can lay hold to what God has promised by our acts of obedience and our faith confession.

You and I can update our lives, conditions, and situations with the spoken Word of God. We can call those things which do not exist as though they did exist (Rom. 4:17). We must believe and SPEAK (2 Cor. 4:13). Our faith is revealed by our actions and our words. If your faith remains in the believing mode, you have only mentally assented or merely wishful thinking. Pastor Mark Hankins said it like this, "In order to win the fight of faith, we must first win the war of words. If our faith is silent, we lose by default." Exactly, we must win the war of words. As God created with the power of his words so we should imitate him and follow his example. We have the power to change our lives and circumstances with our words of faith. Speak to it!

Faith Reminders...

◀ Faith must be in the heart (the Word believed) and in the mouth (the Word spoken).

◀ Believing is only one part of faith.

◀ Positive thinking changes you. A faith confession changes your circumstances.

◀ Faith requires action and believing requires a confession.

◀ The initial use of language was not communication, but creativity.

Make it Personal:
What I learned about faith is...

____

____

____

____

____

____

____

____

____

____

____

____

____

____

____

____

4

My Fight of Faith

Pastor Rod's Testimony...

On December 31, 2012, we celebrated big at our New Year's Eve service. The congregation at NLCC went up with a high praise and exalted the name of the Lord. It was an amazing service that was filled with the presence of God, family and close friends.

Little did I know, our world was getting ready to be shaken like never before. Our faith was getting ready to be tested. My wife and I woke up the next day on January 1,

2013 preparing to go visit my in-laws. As we were loading our vehicle for travel, we got a call. My sister, Marcie, had been rushed to the hospital and it looked like she had a stroke. I was stunned.

In my mind, I was like "What! She's only 28." It was surreal. We were just together last night at the New Year's Eve service. My sister was praising and giving God glory and now she was being rushed to the hospital for a possible stroke. WOW! So we got in our vehicle and proceeded to the hospital. I pulled up and I saw my dad's eyes were swollen from crying. My mom was standing at the emergency room exit outside. I hugged her and she began to weep for her daughter. After I comforted her, I proceeded to go inside the hospital and before I could get in the door; my brother, J-Mack, came out crying and said "Rodney, she doesn't even know who I am." My heart dropped to my stomach.

DON'T GO BY WHAT YOU SEE...

I took several deep breaths and proceeded to see my sister in the emergency room. Before I could get in the room, the

Holy Spirit said, "Don't go by what you see." I got in the room and my sister was lying in the bed with a twisted face, swollen tongue, and a drawn up left arm. The situation looked hopeless. However, the Holy Spirit told me before entering the room "Don't go by what you see." This phrase from the Holy Spirit prepared me for what I was going to see behind the curtain in the emergency room.

At this point, I was hurting. I had an array of emotions and felt like falling apart, but this wasn't the time to fall apart. It was time to fight. We had to fight the good fight of faith for my sister. So I set my feelings aside and leaned over to Marcie and spoke in her ear "My name is Rodney. I'm your brother. If you can hear me, we are going to beat this." Still not able to speak, she nodded her head in agreement.

While holding back the tears because I didn't want her to see me cry, I talked to God in my mind. I told him, "I don't know how you're going to do this, but you're going to get the glory out of this." This was painful. My sister was a good person. She had given her life to Christ and something like this happened to her. However, I was comforted by the Holy Spirit with these words that bad things do happen to good people, but God will make it up to you by causing all things to work together for our good because we love him and are called according to his purpose (Rom. 8:28).

I took a seat next to her bed to comfort her and encourage her to stay in peace. Even as I write this, I'm amazed at how I was comforting my sister and at the same time the Holy Spirit was comforting and holding me together. Truly, the Holy Spirit is a helper and strengthener.

JESUS IS ENOUGH...

While sitting next to my sister in the emergency room, I didn't have any long and eloquent prayers. Honestly, I was lost for words. I didn't have any 7 step plan of how to turn this around. However, I did have and knew the name of Jesus. So I shifted and began to worship and bless God in this painful situation. As I worshipped, I began to see things even the more from God's point of view. God was going to get the glory out of this.

Softly and intelligently (I didn't get crazy in the emergency room and pull out the oil and go to slanging it…LOL), I began to speak the name of Jesus over my sister's body and commanded it to line up to the Scriptures that with the stripes of Jesus she was healed (Isa. 53:5; 1Pet. 2:24). I just kept speaking Jesus to her body. While speaking the name of Jesus to her body, the Holy Spirit kept rehearsing in my hearing "Don't go by what you see. Don't go by what you see." Therefore, I kept speaking Jesus over her and commanded her body to line up to the Word.

Periodically, the medical staff would come in and the doctor informed me that it looked like a stroke based upon the symptoms, but we are running tests to get the exact diagnosis. As soon as they would leave, I would go back into worship and speak the name of Jesus over Marcie's body. At first, nothing was happening in the natural, but I kept worshipping and speaking the name of Jesus. Why, because the name of Jesus is above every name (Phil. 2:9). Therefore, every condition or diagnosis no matter what its name is had to submit to the name of Jesus.

In the emergency room, I worshipped and spoke the name of Jesus. I worshipped and spoke the name of Jesus. I worshipped and spoke the name of Jesus. While worshipping and speaking the name of Jesus, I saw a twisted face come back into alignment. While worshipping and speaking the name of Jesus, I saw a drawn up arm come back to a normal relaxed position. There is POWER in the name of Jesus! When we speak the name of Jesus, every condition, prognosis, diagnosis, and name must bow to the name of Jesus. The name of Jesus is SUPREME! When you don't know what to say, speak the name of Jesus. When the words of prayer don't come to mind, speak the name of Jesus. There is POWER in the name of Jesus.

Jesus is ENOUGH! When we speak the name of Jesus over someone's life, it becomes active intercession. All that Jesus is and represents is released into his or her life at that time. Jesus is the Word made flesh. He is the embodiment of the Word. Whenever the Word is spoken or sent, it will not return void, useless or without accomplishing its purpose. The Word works. In fact, the Scripture says, "He sent His word and healed them and delivered them from their destructions (Psalm 107:20)."

This miraculous healing was the beginning of a journey of healing and restoration for my sister. God proved himself to be faithful throughout the process. I will never forget those moments in the emergency room on January 1, 2013. I will never forget what I learned about God in a painful crisis. It was this crisis that gave birth to positive change in my perspective about God and increased faith in the name that is above every name, the name of Jesus.

You may be facing a crisis or in a crisis right now. To you I say as the Holy Spirit told me, "Don't go by what you see." God is working on your behalf. In the natural, it may appear that nothing is changing or getting better. Don't go by what you see. God is going to get the glory out of this. He is going to turn this bad situation around for your GOOD and for his GLORY. He's going to give you DOUBLE for your trouble (Isa.61:7). Believe it! Expect it! Speak it!

Faith Reminders...

- As concerning faith, don't go by what you see.

- Faith doesn't deny that there is a problem. Faith denies the problem's right to reign in your life.

- Bad things do happen to good people, but God will make it up to us by causing all things to work together for our good because we love him and are called according to his purpose (Rom. 8:28).

- Jesus is ENOUGH!

- The name of Jesus is above every name. Every condition or diagnosis no matter what its name is has to submit to the name of Jesus (Phil.2:9).

- When we worship, it allows us to see things from God's point of view.

- There is POWER in the name of Jesus.

- When the words of prayer don't come to mind, speak the name of Jesus.

- Whenever the Word is spoken or sent, it will not return void, useless or without accomplishing its purpose (Isa.55:11).

◀ He sent His word and healed them and delivered them from their destructions (Psalm 107:20).

MAKE IT PERSONAL:
WHAT I LEARNED ABOUT FAITH IS...

Part III

Declarations

DECLARATIONS

You shall also decide and decree a thing,
and it shall be established for you;
and the light [of God's favor] shall
shine upon your ways.

—JOB 22:28 AMP

5

Scriptures about the tongue...

Say unto them, As truly as I live, saith the Lord, as ye have spoken in mine ears, so will I do to you... (Numbers 14:28)

This book of the law shall not depart out of thy mouth; but thou shalt meditate therein day and night, that thou mayest observe to do according to all that is written therein: for then thou shall make thy way prosperous, and then thou shall have good success. (Joshua 1:8)

Keep your tongue from evil, and your lips from speaking guile. Depart from evil, and do good; seek peace, and pursue it. (Psalm 34:13)

The mouth of the righteous is a well of life, but violence covers the mouth of the wicked. (Proverbs 10:11)

The words of the wicked are to lie in wait for blood: but the mouth of the upright shall deliver them. (Proverbs 12:6)

The wicked is snared by the transgression of his lips; but the just shall come out of trouble. (Proverbs 12:13)

A man shall be satisfied with good by the fruit of his mouth: and the recompense of a man's hands shall be rendered unto him. (Proverbs 12:14)

There is one who speaks like the piercings of a sword, but the tongue of the wise promotes health. The truthful lip shall be established forever, but a lying tongue is but for a moment. (Proverbs 12:18)

Anxiety in the heart of man causes depression, but a good word makes it glad. (Proverbs 12:25)

He who guards his mouth preserves his life, but he who opens wide his lips shall have destruction. (Proverbs 13:3)

A soft answer turns away wrath, but a harsh word stirs up anger. The tongue of the wise uses knowledge rightly, but the mouth of fools pours forth foolishness. (Proverbs 15:1)

A wholesome tongue is a tree of life, but perverseness in it breaks the spirit. (Proverbs 15:4)

A man hath joy by the answer of his mouth: and a word spoken in due season, how good is it! (Proverbs 15:23)

Pleasant words are like a honeycomb, sweetness to the soul and health to the bones. (Proverbs 16:24)

The words of a man's mouth are deep waters; the wellspring of wisdom is a flowing brook. (Proverbs 18:4)

A man's stomach shall be satisfied from the fruit of his mouth, and from the produce of his lips he shall be filled. (Proverbs 18:20)

Death and life are in the power of the tongue, and those who love it will eat its fruit. (Proverbs 18:21)

Whoever guards his mouth and tongue keeps his soul from troubles. (Proverbs 21:23)

The Lord God has given me the tongue of the learned, that I should know how to speak a word in season to him who is weary. (Isaiah 50:4)

For verily I say unto you, that whosoever shall say unto this mountain, be thou removed, and be cast into the sea; and shall not doubt in his heart, but shall believe that those things which he saith shall come to pass; HE SHALL HAVE WHATSOEVER HE SAITH. (Mark 11:23)

Walk in wisdom toward those who are outside, redeeming the time. Let your speech always be with grace, seasoned with salt, that you may know how you ought to answer each one. (Colossians 4:5)

MAKE IT PERSONAL: WHAT I LEARNED ABOUT THE TONGUE IS...

6

I.D.

—

IDENTITY DECLARATIONS...

In Jesus' name, I decree and declare that...

I am a son of God.

I am saved by grace.

I am born of the incorruptible seed.

I am redeemed by the blood of Jesus.

I am forgiven of all my sins.

I am a new creature in Christ.

I am accepted and approved of by God.

I am fearfully and wonderfully made.

I am free from condemnation.

I am strong and victorious through Jesus Christ.

I am complete in Christ.

I am crucified with Christ.

I am alive with Christ.

I am God's masterpiece recreated in Christ Jesus to do good works.

I am the apple of my Father's eye.

I am a joint heir with Jesus.

I am more than a conqueror.

I am the head and not the tail.

I am above and not beneath.

I am delivered from the power of darkness.

I am translated into the kingdom of God.

I am seated in heavenly places in Christ Jesus.

I am blessed with all spiritual blessings in heavenly places.

I am the righteousness of God in Christ.

I am the redeemed declaring my salvation.

I am the forgiven declaring my forgiveness.

I am the friend of God declaring my friendship.

I am the anointed declaring my anointing.

I am the doer of the Word declaring my faith.

I am the empowered declaring my authority.

I am the skillful declaring my skill.

I am the strong declaring my strength.

I am the conqueror declaring my victory.

I am the liberated declaring my freedom.

I am the wise-hearted declaring my wisdom.

I am the blessed of God declaring my favor.

I am the rich declaring my prosperity.

I am the favored declaring my advantage.

I am the healed declaring my healing.

I am the protected declaring my protection.

I am the peacemaker declaring my peace.

I am the thankful declaring my thanksgiving.

By the grace of God I am what I am—1 Cor. 15:10.

MAKE IT PERSONAL:
WHAT I LEARNED ABOUT IDENTITY IS...

FAITH DECLARATIONS...

DECLARING PEACE

The Lord has ordained peace for me and I will not be moved to sudden panic or fear. The peace of God governs my heart and settles and brings to finality any questions that may arise in my mind. *(Isaiah 26:12; Col. 3:15 AMP)*

I have a sound mind. My thoughts are established and agreeable to God's will. *(2 Tim. 1:7 & Proverbs 16:3 AMP)*

I have the mind of Christ, the Messiah, and do hold the thoughts, feelings, and purposes of his heart. *(1 Cor. 2:16 AMP)*

DECLARING THE FAVOR OF GOD

I am satisfied with favor and full of the blessing of the Lord. *(Deut. 33:23)*

I am God's favorite child. He has surrounded me with favor like a shield. Therefore, when people meet me; they come in contact with my favor shield and are inclined to like me, cooperate with me, do good to me, and bless me. *(Psalm 5:12)*

The favor of God rests upon me and establishes the works of my hands. *(Psalm 90:17)*

I, like Jesus, am increasing in wisdom and favor with God and men. *(Luke 2:52)*

God is causing all grace (every favor and earthly blessing) to come to me in abundance so that I am equipped and ready to do what needs to be done. *(2 Cor. 9:8 AMP)*

Declaring my Blessings

The Lord is multiplying me a thousand times more than what I am and blessing me as he has promised. *(Deut. 1:11)*

Because I obey God's voice, I am being overtaken by the blessings. *(Deut. 28:1-2)*

The Lord loads me daily with benefits and many blessings are given to me because I trust the Lord. *(Psalm 68:19; Psalm 40:4 TLB)*

The blessing of the Lord makes me rich and there is no sorrow with it. *(Proverbs 10:22)*

God is causing all grace (every favor and earthly blessing) to come to me in abundance so that I am equipped and ready to do what needs to be done. *(2 Cor. 9:8 AMP)*

I am redeemed from the curse of the law that the blessing of Abraham may come upon me. *(Galatians 3:13-14)*

Declaring my Healing

It is the Lord who heals me and with his stripes I am healed. *(Exodus 15:26; Isaiah 53:5; & 1 Peter 2:24)*

Because I serve the Lord, he blesses my bread and water. He takes sickness from the midst of me. *(Exodus 23:25)*

Because I have made the Lord my dwelling place, no evil shall come near me nor shall any plague come near my residence. *(Psalm 91:9-10)*

The Lord heals me of all my diseases and renews my youth. *(Psalm 103:3, 5)*

I shall not die, but live and declare the works of the Lord. *(Psalm 118:17)*

The Lord restores my health and heals me of all my wounds. *(Jeremiah 30:17)*

The Lord makes an utter end to it and this affliction will not arise the second time. *(Nahum 1:9)*

Because Jesus took my infirmities and bore my sicknesses in his own body, I don't have to. I am healed. *(Matthew 8:17)*

Declaring my Increase

The Lord shall multiply me a thousand times more and bless me as he has promised. *(Deut. 1:11)*

The Lord gives me that which is good and my land yields its increase. *(Psalm 85:12)*

The Lord is mindful of me. He will bless me and give me and my children increase. *(Psalm 115:12, 14)*

Declaring my Prosperity

I decree and declare that God has given me the power to get wealth. *(Deut. 8:18)*

Because I obey and serve God, I shall spend my days in prosperity and my years in pleasure. *(Job 36:11)*

I decree and declare that God has pleasure in my prosperity. *(Psalm 35:27)*

I am a giver. Through men, it is given back to me pressed down, shaken together, making room for more and running over into my life. *(Luke 6:38)*

As my soul prospers, I shall prosper in all things and be in good health. *(3 John 1:2)*

Declaring Good Things

Because I walk upright, no good thing will God withhold from me. *(Psalm 84:11)*

For me, God sends blessings of good things to meet me, makes me to be blessed and a blessing forever and makes me exceedingly glad with the joy of his presence. *(Psalm 21:3a, 6 AMP)*

Declaring my Times

My times are in God's hands and he makes all things beautiful in his time for me. *(Psalm 31:15 & Eccl.3:11)*

Wisdom and knowledge shall be the stability of my times. *(Isaiah 33:6)*

DECLARING MY REIGN

I have received the gift of righteousness and I reign in life as a king through Jesus Christ. *(Romans 5:17 AMP)*

DECLARING MY WISDOM

Christ is my wisdom and because I fear the Lord; he will teach me how to choose the best. *(1 Cor. 1:30 & Psalm 25:12 TLB)*

Wisdom and knowledge shall be the stability of my times. *(Isaiah 33:6)*

DECLARING MY CREATION

Because I am in Christ, I am a new creation. Old things have passed away and all things have become new. *(2 Cor. 5:17)*

I am God's workmanship. I've been created in Christ Jesus to do good works. *(Ephesians 2:10)*

Declaring my Protection

God is my hiding place. He preserves me from trouble and surrounds me with songs of deliverance. *(Psalm 32:7)*

Because I fear the Lord, the angel of the Lord guards and surrounds me. *(Psalm 34:7)*

Because I have made the Lord my dwelling place, no evil shall come near me nor shall any plague come near my residence. *(Psalm 91:9-10)*

I have divine protection. God's angels watch over me wherever I go. *(Psalm 91:11)*

The Lord is my confidence and keeps my foot from being caught. *(Proverbs 3:26)*

No weapon formed against me shall prosper. *(Isaiah 54:17)*

I have authority over all the power of the enemy and nothing shall by any means hurt me. *(Luke 10:19)*

Declaring my Help

God is my refuge and strength. He is my very present help in trouble. *(Psalm 46:1)*

You are my strength and shield. Because my heart trusts you, I have help in every area of my life. *(Psalm 28:7)*

I look up because my help comes from the Lord. *(Psalm 121:1-2)*

Declaring Household Salvation

I decree and declare that as for me and my house; we will serve the Lord. My children are for signs and wonders unto the Lord. All the members of my household are saved, delivered, filled with the Spirit and walking in the will of God. *(Josh.24:15; Isa.8:18; Acts 2:38)*

Declaring Perfect Timing

I decree and declare that I am always in the right place, at the right time; connecting with the right people. *(Eccl. 9:11c NLT)*

MAKE IT PERSONAL:
WHAT I LEARNED ABOUT FAITH IS...

about the authors

FOR OVER 20 YEARS, this dynamic, multigifted life changer has been equipping people to discover destiny, maximize potential and to use their lives to make an eternal difference in the world. He is a highly respected preacher, relationship coach, mentor and a speaker who is known for "*keeping it real.*"

RODNEY D. ROBERTSON is the founder of New Life Christian Center and Global Impact Fellowship. He is also an author of best sellers such as *Free to Be Me!, How to Keep a Good Man, You are Not the Mistake* and *The Power of Personal Vision*. He is married to his beautiful wife, LaKeida Robertson. They reside in Louisiana.

LESTER E. DALE JR., has been preaching the Gospel and changing lives through faith for over 20 years. His mantra is "faith overrides every existing fact." He is a highly respected prophet. He is the Senior Pastor of Faith Temple Ministries and the founder and overseer of Word of Faith Fellowship in Mobile, AL. His passion is to equip leaders to lead with excellence and to impact the next generation. He resides in Alabama.

other books
BY RODNEY D. ROBERTSON...

ISBN: 978-0-615-18698-6

A good man is hard to find. In this day and time, a good man is a rare commodity. Inside this best seller, you will discover the secrets to keeping a good man without the help of tricks, schemes, games, and love potions.

You will discover love solutions that will reveal what a good man wants and how you can keep him. If you're already married, your love skills will be sharpened. If you're a lady in waiting, you will be equipped with meaningful insights for the good man that is on the way. *Get ready to enjoy more of life, love, and a lasting connection with your good man.*

**Volume Discount Available

ISBN: 978-0-615-26195-9

You are not the mistake you made! Inside this life changing book, Rodney will show you how to make a comeback from the place where you've fallen. Through his message of hope and restoration, you will find out that

God still loves you, he stands ready to forgive you and you can get up again.

Inside *You are Not the Mistake*, you will learn things like:

- How to find life after the mistake,

- How to forget it and move on,

- How to worship your way to wholeness,

- How to get free from the guilt of the past and so MUCH MORE.

It is your time to get up and walk in your destiny. It doesn't matter if you have fallen one time or 101 times. You aren't what you did. Though a just man falls seven times, he will arise again (Proverbs 24:16). Get ready to receive God's forgiveness, healing, the power to forgive yourself, and the strength to walk in victory every day. **You are Not the Mistake!**

**Volume Discount Available

ISBN: 978-0-578-07043-8

Whether you are a businessperson, an employee, a domestic engineer, a student, or a governmental official, Rodney D. Robertson will explain how you can make your dreams a reality and experience ultimate success through discovering the *Power of Personal Vision.*

Get ready to discover your purpose in life. Understand why personal vision is essential to your personal growth and success. Discover the keys you'll need to fulfill your life's vision. Develop a plan of action for realizing your personal vision and so much MORE.

**Volume Discount Available

All titles available online at:

www.amazon.com

www.rodneyrobertson.org

or Contact us at:

Impact Publishing, LLC

Attn: Publisher

PO Box 74610

Baton Rouge, LA 70874

Email: impactpublishing@ymail.com

also available from Impact Publishing, LLC

ISBN: 978-0-578-02206-2

Inside *How to Recognize a GOOD Man*, LaKeida will share with you her experiences combined with divine wisdom on how to recognize a good man, the value of knowing who you are, and the power of knowing if the man you're considering is a part of your destiny. Get ready to be empowered! Get ready to be enlightened! There is a GOOD man that God has prepared for you and LaKeida wants to help you to recognize him.

**Volume Discount Available

Available online at:

www.rodneyrobertson.org

or Contact us at:

Impact Publishing, LLC

Attn: Publisher

PO Box 74610

Baton Rouge, LA 70874

Email: impactpublishing@ymail.com

contact information

WHETHER YOU RECEIVED *SPEAK TO IT!* as a gift, borrowed it from a friend or purchased it yourself, we're glad you read it. We hope that you will share this book and its message with your family and friends.

Contact Information

If you're interested in writing the authors, wish to receive free newsletters, would like information about their speaking engagements or would like to invite Rodney or Lester to speak at an event you are hosting, please visit their websites or send your written correspondence to the addresses listed below:

STAY CONNECTED WITH RODNEY:

Rodney D. Robertson

PO Box 74610

Baton Rouge, LA 70874

Friend Rodney at **www.facebook.com/rodney.d.robertson**

Follow Rodney on **www.twitter.com/rodneyrobertson**

Instagram: **rodneydrobertson**

www.rodneyrobertson.org

www.newlifecctr.com

STAY CONNECTED WITH LESTER:

Lester E. Dale

3210 First Ave.

Mobile, AL 36617

Friend Lester at **www.facebook.com/pastorlester**

Follow Lester on **www.twitter.com/lesterE36**

Instagram: **lesterdalejr**

www.ingramcontent.com/pod-product-compliance
Lightning Source LLC
Chambersburg PA
CBHW061038050726
47592CB00004B/1490